TIMELESS BY DESIGN

TIMELESS BY DESIGN

DESIGNING ROOMS WITH COMFORT, STYLE,
AND A SENSE OF HISTORY

NINA FARMER

WRITTEN WITH ANDREW SESSA

FOREWORD BY MITCHELL OWENS

Rizzoli
NEW YORK

New York · Paris · London · Milan

FOR QUINN & COLETTE:

I love you more than
the earth, stars, sun, and moon.

CONTENTS

FOREWORD

MITCHELL OWENS

Design has no rules, only possibilities, and most importantly, no boundaries—especially when it comes to styles, materials, or geographic inspirations. Such is the viewpoint of Nina Farmer, a Boston-based interior designer whom I instantly became an admirer of when I met her several years ago during a trip to Morocco.

Visitors to that North African country can be overwhelmed by its aesthetic riches, in much the same way that travelers to museums and cathedrals famously grow dizzy with the symptoms of the delirium known as Stendhal syndrome. "I was in a sort of ecstasy," the phenomenon's namesake, nineteenth-century French writer Stendhal, recalled of his first trip to Florence, Italy, in 1817. "I had palpitations of the heart, what in Berlin they call 'nerves.' Life was drained from me. I walked with the fear of falling."

Nina, on the other hand, embraced every bit of Morocco's beauty without a single faltering step or moment of weakness. Every new sight was another opportunity to be inspired, another chance to take home and incorporate into her projects what she had seen, heard, touched, and smelled. It is the same with every culture, past or present, into which she dives and from which she has created a rich professional vocabulary that is showcased in the residences featured in the pages of *Timeless by Design*.

One room may display an assortment of rugged Tamegroute pottery on a sleek mid-century table. Another may feature a Regency-style chaise longue upholstered in a graphic fabric that speaks of Africa. An angular Chandigarh writing chair from the 1950s, designed by architect Pierre Jeanneret for Indian civil servants, may sidle up to an opulent Victorian staircase. Nina accumulates treasures with the heart of a connoisseur and the mind of a curator, and then she assembles them into inviting spaces where the marriage of textures, patterns, materials, and shapes seems destined rather than decreed.

Her homes for clients, as well as for herself, are collected environments where elegance meets bohemia, where smooth meets nubby, and, most of all, where there meets here and then meets now.

OPPOSITE: The primary suite of a 1928 residence in pastoral Westport, Connecticut, takes style cues from the Mediterranean elements of the original exterior, in particular its terra-cotta roof. The newly added wooden beams and deep-red color of the bedroom ceiling create an old-world atmosphere, while an antique Regency chaise, vintage sconces, and a rattan floor lamp combine in a cozy reading nook whose style spans eras and aesthetics. The Moroccan-inspired wool-silk rug is custom.

INTRODUCTION

Though the path to my career as an interior designer was a bit of a circuitous one, I've always felt at home with design—and with history.

I grew up in suburban Connecticut, not far from New York City, surrounded by houses built over the previous two-hundred-plus years, in aesthetics ranging from Colonial to contemporary, Greek Revival to shingle style. Though neither of my parents had formal design training, they both had passions for architecture, decorating, and art that I very much inherited. When I was three, they designed and built a new house for our family, where they raised me and my brother until we went off to college. My mother likes to remind me that I was on her hip for the whole process, watching attentively (though, apparently, not yet picking out fabric swatches).

During my childhood, I don't think we missed a single Kips Bay Decorator Show House in Manhattan. And there was always new work in our house by an artisan or artist that my parents had recently discovered and wanted to support: a piece of furniture or a painting they had spotted while traveling abroad—or when out and about closer to home—that they just had to have.

My mother was born in Finland, and some of my first design memories revolve around our summer visits back to her native Scandinavia. There, I was charmed by her family's little red centuries-old seaside cottage, which sat at the end of a dirt path, and I marveled at the well-preserved old-world opulence of Stockholm—making notes in my mental sketchbook of things I'd never seen in America.

Thanks to these trips, I learned early that the world is bigger and history longer than they might have seemed from my suburban bedroom. I came to feel part of a larger story.

After majoring in biology during college in New Orleans—a place that wears its layers of history and mix of cultures more vividly, more intriguingly, than anywhere else in America—I flirted with the idea of going to medical school and then with the possibility of a career in public health.

Ultimately, though, I decided to pursue what had always been my primary passion—apparent to anyone who knew me, even if I had long thought

OPPOSITE: Abaca grass cloth wallpaper panels hand-painted with custom designs hang on the living room walls of a 1940s house in Concord, Massachusetts. I commissioned a henna artist to create the motifs, providing an additional layer of texture and craft in a room where other artisanal elements include a vintage Tabriz rug and a fireplace surround clad in antique azulejos tiles from Portugal.

medicine was my calling—and I dove into the world of architecture and decoration. I attended interior design school in New York and then moved to Boston, where my husband was about to begin his medical fellowship. I hadn't previously spent much time in the city, but I found myself immediately drawn to its deep aesthetic history, just as I had been in Stockholm, New Orleans, and Connecticut.

We settled into an 1850s townhouse in Beacon Hill, one of the city's oldest neighborhoods, where the narrow cobblestone streets, gas lamps, and brownstone buildings transport you back in time and across the Atlantic to England. The redesign of our own new home became my first project in our new hometown, serving first as a learning laboratory and later as a calling card as I set up my business.

While the exteriors of Beacon Hill's rowhouses have landmark protection, preventing owners from making changes to their facades, you're free to do anything you want inside. At the time I redid the interiors of our house, many people stuck with decor that hewed to tradition—dutifully restoring plaster moldings and leaded-glass windows, and choosing patterns, colors, furniture, art, and antiques from the period of their homes' construction. Or, they abandoned tradition entirely, stripping out original architectural details and then decorating with a sleek contemporary point of view.

I was looking for something different. I didn't want decor that was such a literal, direct match for the original architecture, but I didn't want to rebel against it completely either. Thinking you have to go entirely in one direction or the other, I realized, is a false choice.

Instead, I used history as a guide, preserving the decadent details that gave the house character and a sense of grandeur—the deeply carved crown moldings and ceiling medallions, the scale and size of the rooms, the colorful tilework fireplace surrounds and marble mantels—then used these to inspire new interior architectural elements that I added in to bridge the gap between now and then. From there, I selected a mix of furniture, art, and accessories from a variety of my favorite periods and places. Creating rooms that looked collected, I filled each space with pieces that could have been acquired over time from around the world, then lovingly arranged them to create a richly layered aesthetic. The result is a timeless look and feel that lets my family live as comfortably, and as well, as we might have in a brand-new twenty-first-century home that had been purpose built to our contemporary needs.

What I did for my own home apparently struck a chord with the people who eventually became my clients. I soon had more projects to redo Beacon Hill townhouses with landmark status, followed by commissions for the interiors of historic houses in greater Boston and throughout New England. I clearly was on to something.

These early commissions confirmed two things that I'd long suspected: every house has a story worth telling, and every homeowner has an important story to tell, too. The pleasure—and the power—of interior design, I came to understand, comes from weaving these stories together and doing so in ways that are as seamless as they are lovely to look at, as timeless as they are timely.

Today, not all of my work finds me helping clients with houses built a century or more ago. But some combination of a building's history and the story of a home's owners always provides the jumping-off point for what I do.

In my work, I've learned to be inspired by history but never constrained by it. And that's given me the

OPPOSITE: Combining past and present, I selected vintage sconces to flank a new mirror fitted with antique glass in a late-nineteenth-century Victorian house in a suburb just west of Boston.

freedom to intertwine aesthetics from the past and the present, gathering objects and ideas both from the here and now and from around the world and across time. The rooms that result from this way of designing are as unique as the stories of the people who occupy them—and of the houses and neighborhoods, historic and otherwise, in which they sit.

My signature mix of past and present creates a sense of timelessness that makes the environments I design feel personal, warm, and welcoming. You recognize something about these rooms, and something of yourself in them, too. Pieces with a sense of age—classical lines and a bit of patina—somehow always feel familiar. They trigger, perhaps, some pleasing sense of nostalgia, though we may not know for what exactly, reminding us of generations that came before. Modern and contemporary items, meanwhile, position us in the present day, providing us with a sense that we're part of a timeline that's ongoing, and always stretching forward. The overall result of this combination is the soothing, reassuring feeling that comes from being at home with history while living decidedly in the twenty-first century.

It is my great joy, and privilege, to help my clients see the beauty and value of classical and traditional architecture, and to allow them to make it work with how they want to live today. This book, I hope, will share that with you, too. In the following pages, I'll illustrate the various ways I think about combining old and new in my interiors, and then show how it all comes together to create the places we call home.

RIGHT: Though filled with antique furnishings and vintage art, the formal, parlor-level living room of my own home—an 1850s brownstone in Boston's historic Beacon Hill neighborhood—is anything but stuffy. Here, my daughters and I share a relaxed moment on the custom wool-cashmere-upholstered chesterfield sofa I had made to complement 1920s French Art Deco chairs from Paris and an oil painting that my artist mother made specifically for the room.

THREADS OF INSPIRATION

CELEBRATING THE PAST

One of the things I love most about working on old houses is the way their style and details can evoke a specific sense of time and place: the Mediterranean flavor of a hundred-year-old estate in suburban Connecticut (see page 125) suggests the countryside of Southern France or Greece at the turn of the last century; the hand-carved woodwork of a 1904 English Arts & Crafts–style home outside of Boston (see page 145) recalls the work of William Morris in the United Kingdom and the renaissance of artisanal methods it inspired in the wake of the Industrial Revolution. These houses immediately provide something to grab on to, a spot to start designing from.

To put it another way, the past is always present in a historic home. The trick is figuring out how best, and how much, to celebrate what came before.

For every project, I start by making something of an informal inventory of a house's strengths (carefully hand-rendered details, for example) and its challenges (a floor plan comprising a warren of too-small rooms, say). Then, I design in a manner that elevates what works and lets go of what doesn't, making choices about what we should directly preserve and what might better serve as broad inspiration to inform the decor.

But it's not just a house's historic architecture that helps me honor its past. The addition of antiques and vintage art—perhaps from a home's original period, but well beyond, too—is also very much part of the story.

OPPOSITE: The impressive architecture of this 1904 Arts & Crafts house led me to select furnishings with enough substance and style to hold their own with the beautifully carved original woodwork. In the entry, that meant selecting a monumental chest from Blackman Cruz and an iconic Pierre Jeanneret Chandigarh chair.

HISTORIC ARCHITECTURE

Architecture is where interior design begins, especially when you have a historic house. I'm always looking to create balance between the architectural envelope of a home and the decor and furnishings that finish it. That doesn't mean if you've got an 1850s Federal brownstone, like mine (see page 75), you should think of it as a museum, remaining slavishly true to its period and style. I want to create aesthetic harmony, yes, but I'm also interested in developing a certain intriguing tension between old and new.

To achieve this, I like to focus on unique original elements that help give a house its particular character: a certain molding profile, a floor motif, a beautifully glazed tile, the curve of a stair stringer—artisanal details that wouldn't, or couldn't, be crafted the same way today. And then I honor them through various methods.

In some places, like the formerly crumbling plaster crown moldings of my own Beacon Hill living room, that might mean restoring details to their original ornate grandeur in their intended location. In other places, it might mean using a beautiful, intact element to inspire something else, something more. The hue of the existing, mid-nineteenth-century glazed tiles surrounding the fireplaces in my house went on to inspire the color palette in two of the rooms: blue-green accents in the living area, pale yellows in the primary suite.

Historic homes offer much more than just enticing details like these, of course. They have a wonderful sense of scale and proportion, too, especially in their public and entertaining spaces. Today, architecture and design can be quite tactical, even utilitarian. We think more about what spaces we need to have in order to get through our daily routine, rather than how high ceilings, good proportions, and a generous sense of space can make you feel.

One of the greatest design opportunities in older houses is in finding the perfect balance between historic formality and present-day functionality. Although it's the richness of original period details and the grandeur of high ceilings and large rooms that attract me and my clients to the atmospheric period homes I work on, these elements can also present a bit of challenge. They sometimes add up to an atmosphere that feels more fussy than friendly, more grandiose than gracious.

There's a risk that these houses, if decorated in ways that play into their original period too literally, can make you feel like they're untouchable, only appropriate if you're hosting a formal dinner or cocktail party—and dressed for the part. I find that my design schemes need to carefully cut against this possibility by including materials, textures, patterns, colors, and furniture that read as more friendly than foreboding. Doing so allows each older home I work on to find its own particular sense of twenty-first-century refinement, one that's better aligned with the relaxed way we all want to live and entertain now.

OPPOSITE: The Mediterranean exterior of the 1928 Westport house, as well as its three acres of mature gardens, suggested an array of design references from a century, or more, ago. The architecture's stone walls, recessed windows, wooden shutters, and iron grates inspired many of my choices for the interior, not least the palette of colors, patterns, and materials.

ABOVE AND OPPOSITE: This neoclassical 1910 residence just outside Boston impresses
with the formality of its traditional architecture and its hilltop setting. My clients and
I wanted to celebrate this historic grandeur and sense of elegance both inside and out.

CELEBRATING THE PAST

ABOVE: When decorating the powder room of a Victorian house, I selected pieces that echoed the geometry of the room's original leaded glass window: a graphic, painted grass cloth wallpaper and a curvaceous pendant light wrapped in handwoven wire fabric. A sleek brass-framed mirror and picture light keep things balanced.
OPPOSITE: For the family room, with its remarkably well-preserved woodwork, I designed vintage-inspired custom furnishings that look as if the clients' family had collected them over the course of decades, or even centuries.

CELEBRATING THE PAST

PERIOD ANTIQUES

Whether or not a house's existing architecture and design details exactly suit my clients' taste, or my own, my first instinct is always to see if we can make them work. Not everything is worth saving, of course, but when possible, I tailor my plans for furniture, finishes, and fixtures to build around what came before.

I find that the more historic detail a house gives you, the more there is to back away from, to prevent the house from becoming too formal, museum like, or a facsimile of the past. The less you're given, the more you can lean in, with decor that feels of a piece. The most interesting, compelling, and timeless interiors are not the historic clones but the new hybrids.

For me, there's no better way to create this sort of timeless hybrid than by incorporating antique and vintage items into the furniture mix. This doesn't mean sticking with pieces true to a house's original era. I find that items from almost any past period can offer an instant feeling of warmth, age, and patina. Antiques encourage your mind to wander.

You wonder where a dramatically carved console table might be from, who might have crafted it, and who owned it. Vintage items have lived lives of their own long before they came into your life, and that instills in them a certain magical alchemy.

I often gravitate toward Art Deco because of its clean-lined interpretation of traditional styles and celebration of craft in modern-feeling ways. Antiques from this era elegantly bridge what can be a rather cavernous gap between a contemporary way of living and the classical vernacular architecture of the Federal, Victorian, shingle style, and Arts & Crafts houses my studio most often works on. Equally simpatico are mid-twentieth-century European pieces, especially those from Scandinavia.

Part of the appeal of using antiques is also the thrill of the hunt. I get a particular rush when I find the perfect vintage piece for a space after a long search, especially when it has a rich past. I love to share that with clients, so that the item's history becomes part of the story of their home.

OPPOSITE: In the primary bedroom of the Westport house, a mid-century modern ceramic lamp by Einar Johansen and a vintage Kai Blomquist glass vase from Finland sit atop an antique Charles Dudouyt desk.

PREVIOUS PAGES: Designing a home for an ardent collector of Art Deco furniture—a passion I share—was a particular treat. The living room features such pieces as French barrel-backed chairs and an Italian enamel side table adorned with zodiac symbols. **ABOVE:** The den's mid-twentieth-century Italian credenza is attributed to Vittorio Dassi. **RIGHT:** Murano glass lamps flank the sofa. I based the custom rug on a 1920s design by Émile-Jacques Ruhlmann.

CELEBRATING THE PAST

ABOVE AND OPPOSITE: For the primary suite's dressing area and bathroom, my client asked me to borrow the aesthetic of Claridge's, the historic London hotel celebrated as a masterpiece of Art Deco design. Cerused oak cabinetry, Grigio Carnico and Calacatta Vagli marbles, and fluted glass-and-nickel wall sconces did just the trick.

VINTAGE ART

Integrating older artworks into an interior provides many of the same benefits as designing with antiques and historic architectural details. By adding elements from outside our own time—and the time of a house's original construction—we can create a sense of timelessness.

I have a personal soft spot for the look of the mid-twentieth-century European paintings my grandparents long collected and eventually gave to me, several of which hang on the walls in my living room now. Their rich palettes and unfettered style, which falls somewhere between Impressionism and Modernism, speak to me. I feel at home with them.

When homeowners don't come to me with their own heirlooms or with a particular style or period of art that speaks to them—and most don't—we almost always still look for older pieces to display, often from the same timeframe my grandparents favored. There's just something about this period that brings visual interest and impact to a space without overwhelming it.

Even if you can't pinpoint a painting's exact era or aesthetic, you can still usually tell it's not from today. Maybe it's the palette, or the technique, or the patina. Because of that, these works provide a sense of authenticity. They help create the feeling that a house wasn't decorated all at once but rather came together over the space of decades, maybe even generations.

That, in turn, generates an atmosphere of warmth and, even, belonging. Together with the other historic layers I employ, older art makes us feel like we're part of something larger than our own particular era and location, and that of our houses' origins. These elements provide a sense of continuity with the past as well as a sense of movement through time, into the present and beyond.

OPPOSITE: A mid-twentieth-century painting by Vietnamese artist Vu Cao Dam—who trained under European masters at Hanoi's École des Beaux Arts d'Indochine and later settled in Paris—strikes just the right note in the office of a Beacon Hill townhouse that shows off a range of century- and globe-spanning influences.

In the entry of a neoclassical house, the loose, vigorous brushwork and bright accents of a late-twentieth-century painting by French Expressionist Bernard Lorjou provide intriguing contrast to the room's overall sense of tradition and formality.

EXPLORING
THE WORLD

The original well-to-do owners of the mid-to-late nineteenth-century and early twentieth-century houses I work on were often great travelers. These grand tourists collected objects, ideas, and inspiration everywhere they went. In the rooms I design, I endeavor to echo this spirit of wander-lust—and the acquisitiveness that came with it. Cultivating an atmosphere of globe-trotting world-liness has proven key to creating interiors with a collected, timeless look.

Most often, this means adding furniture, textiles, and design motifs that I've gathered on trips from Morocco to Scandinavia, from the Mediterranean to India, and Central America, too, as well as via armchair travel through books and films to places well beyond New England.

Using a Rajasthani block print with a tile pattern from a Marrakech palace, or adding, say, a three-legged Ethiopian stool, Greek-inspired painted ceiling beams, or Charlotte Perriand chairs from a Paris flea market not only creates visual interest. It also helps spin a rich, sophisticated story of style and substance, much like the careful mixing of time periods described in the previous section. Just as I blend eras to prevent an interior from looking like a time capsule, I select elements from different locations to keep rooms from appearing stuck in one particular place. Instead, they feel like they are part of the broader world and a larger community—and they're warmer and more welcoming as a result.

OPPOSITE: To design this beach house—on the island of Martha's Vineyard, just off the coast of Cape Cod—I borrowed elements from the seaside Mediterranean aesthetics of Greece and Spain, as well as pieces from Mozambique and Morocco.
FOLLOWING PAGES: In the family room of another home, an Indonesian carving the homeowners bought on their travels hangs over the fireplace.

THE GLOBAL BAZAAR

When I look around my own Beacon Hill townhouse, my eye lands on and lingers over items I bought while traveling or that were brought back for me by others: bronze Benin sculptures from present-day Nigeria, a portrait of an Indian maharaja from Jaipur, hand-blown glassware from Murano, and many more. Most of these captivating things are artisanally made, revealing the hand of the craftspeople who created them.

Each feels like it has a backstory—the Murano glasses, for example, bear the family crest of the maker, who grew up in one of the most fabulous palazzos on the Grand Canal—and backstory is exactly what I'm trying to give every room I design. People talk about a house telling a story, but I want those that I decorate to contain an entire anthology of interwoven tales.

To that Mediterranean-style Connecticut estate from the 1920s, for example, I added ancient carved Maltese limestone, decorative painting inspired by a vineyard in Portugal, and vintage Moroccan Tamegroute ceramics. Every house—every individual room, even—should have a series of objects and elements like these, pieces that seem to speak to you, and to others who enter the space.

On my travels, I am always on the hunt for incredible finds, and I've gotten pretty good at homing in on what a place is known for—wood carving in Colombia, block prints in India's north, zellige tiles in northern Africa. I then spend my trips learning about quality, detail, and construction in order to seek out and find the best iterations and examples of these items, and to see them actually being made, too.

The locations I gravitate toward and pull from tend to be older societies, places that wear their patina with great pride. The cultures in these destinations still emphasize and value the handmade in ways that we don't as much in the States anymore. We used to, however, and that's why artisanally produced pieces from around the world can work so well in historic American homes. They exhibit the same attention to detail, materiality, and craft.

When I find people using their hands and making things from scratch, I feel a responsibility, almost a moral imperative, to support them. Many are family businesses, and we need to buy from, honor, and elevate them. If not, we're going to lose them.

OPPOSITE: The cultured, cultivated mix of international materials and elements in the powder room of this Mediterranean-inspired Westport house includes Moroccan zellige tile on the walls as well as a sink hand-carved from ancient Maltese limestone and based on a European antique.

OPPOSITE: Departing from the existing Arts & Crafts aesthetic of the original house, this kitchen serves up a look reminiscent of Art Deco bistros and brasseries in Paris. **ABOVE:** Nestled into the arched alcove of a plaster wall, the zellige-tiled bar recalls the curves of the stucco architecture of Corsica.

INTERNATIONAL INSPIRATIONS

When I travel, even if I'm not shopping for physical objects, I'm always shopping for ideas—on the lookout, iPhone camera at the ready, for interesting patterns, materials, and motifs that inspire me and make me want to find a place for them in future projects. And I find the more I travel, the more I catch the right details. There's something about being outside of our usual environment that heightens our awareness and elevates our senses.

Starting with my childhood summers spent visiting my mother's family in Scandinavia, travel has helped me see the world with fresh eyes. On those early trips to Finland, it was all about the simplicity of the red-painted wood exterior of the seaside cottage where we stayed, with its board-and-batten walls and exposed shelving filled with Arabia dishware and handwoven baskets. I've come to reference this aesthetic time and time again when looking to impart a sense of simplicity to a decor, especially in waterfront houses.

The particular details I'm drawn to when I travel, and that I find most useful in interiors, often have a graphic element. They feel contemporary even though they're rendered in traditional materials using artisanal means: geometric stone and tile floor patterns finished and fitted together by hand, deeply carved wood doors and moldings with apparent chisel marks, and high-contrast chevrons, lattices, and abstracted florals in handwoven textiles.

Rarely do I exactly re-create these motifs—though that does happen from time to time. More often, I change the scale or the color to make something feel even more modern or more connected to the place in which I'm designing. Similarly, I generally avoid designing a room that's an homage to one particular locale. It's proven much more successful for me to weave in elements from all over, uniting them by palette, perhaps, but also letting them stand in contrast to one another, to better create visual interest.

For a project in an English-inspired mid-nineteenth-century Beacon Hill townhouse (see page 105), for example, I designed a rug using a *chintamani* motif dating to the Ottoman Empire. But I reimagined it in a rich saffron, indigo, and cognac palette that felt bolder than the original, and therefore fresher and more current. And in the Mediterranean-inspired suburban Connecticut home, I created a custom mosaic-tile floor that riffed on a centuries-old Italian design, reimagining the coloration and scale to fit the needs of the space, and to allow the design to take on a life all its own.

OPPOSITE: The Anglophile tendencies of the owners of a Beacon Hill townhouse led me to pursue an aesthetic with a decidedly English sense of color, pattern, and layering, with some elements borrowed directly from my clients' favorite London hotels. For the moss-hued, board-and-batten dining room, I even selected an artwork by British artist Tom Hammick. The custom rug's design is based on an Ottoman *chintamani* motif.

I channeled the spare, sophisticated, and lovingly finished architecture and design of many centuries-old European churches and monasteries for several spaces in the Westport home. **OPPOSITE:** The mudroom's custom corner bench resembles a church pew—but in the most comfortable way possible. **ABOVE:** In a kitchen corner, a Josef Hoffmann chair and brass-footed sycamore table sit in front of a wall clad in the same fieldstone as the house's exterior.

A SENSE OF PLACE

In addition to incorporating a variety of individual furnishings and assorted motifs and patterns inspired by global travels—both real and imagined—I will, from time to time, seek to channel the overall atmosphere of a particular location in the homes I design. Sometimes, this comes about at the request of clients who have a passion for a singular destination; other times, it's the result of something suggested by a house's exterior architectural style or by the home's unique setting. Whatever their raison d'être, these uniquely immersive environments take inspiration not just from the aesthetic style of a place but also from an almost ineffable sense of the lifestyle there.

Consider, for example, the English-inflected Beacon Hill brownstone, which I designed for confirmed Anglophiles who loved spending time in London and the surrounding countryside. I wanted them to have a home that celebrated the look and feel of this favorite destination. And so I sourced pieces, antique and new, from the UK, and, even more important, I leaned into the whimsical, colorful, layered aesthetic of the best British interiors.

Elsewhere, at a sprawling shingle-style Gilded Age "cottage" in coastal Maine, the immediate surroundings, as well as the easy, summertime holiday vibe, demanded attention. The craggy coast's moss-covered boulders, the forested lands beyond, and the broad sea views guided my palette. And a feeling of remoteness—being off the grid in a place that people of means had been coming to for more than a century to be with family and friends—led me to combine the relaxed with the refined. Here, summer-celebrating elements, like wicker and rattan, waxed linen, and large-scale floral prints mix with tufted velvet upholstery in large, entertaining-ready yet cozy spaces.

A looser sense of place defines the interiors of the Connecticut house, where a Mediterranean-style stone facade inspired my aesthetic journey through Spain, Greece, Italy, Morocco, and France. And, at my own weekend house on Martha's Vineyard ("Island Beauty," page 221), the simple 1950s bungalow's impressive private beach led me to evoke seaside settings from Corsica and Crete to California.

When a sense of place really works, a house feels both at one with its particular locale and at home in the larger world.

OPPOSITE: In the living room of the Beacon Hill townhouse, another work by British artist Tom Hammick hangs above the couch. I selected the fabric on the chair because it reminded me of a pattern I'd noticed in an English country house.

LIVING IN
THE PRESENT

No matter how much my designs for historic houses are borne out of a deeply felt desire to honor the past, I am always guided by the knowledge that I am creating space for busy twenty-first-century families living busy twenty-first-century lives. The interiors I create must make it easy for them to feel at home in the current day and age.

Our homes are our most personal, sacred places, where we make some of our greatest memories, celebrate life's milestones, and host our closest friends and family. No one wants an interior that asks them to play second fiddle to centuries-old architecture.

A historic home has to work in harmony with its current occupants' needs, just as it did with those of its original residents.

The best strategy for making that possible, I've found, is to have an open mind. Considering (and reconsidering), evaluating (and reevaluating) what history has given helps me to identify opportunities instead of challenges, and to see inspiring details and charming quirks instead of hard-to-overcome oddities. Out of these discovered opportunities can come the creative, contemporary design and decorating solutions that bridge a house from the past to the present, and carry it into the future.

OPPOSITE: Designed for staff, the original kitchens of century-old houses have few features required by twenty-first-century families, especially homeowners who love to cook and entertain. As a result, I often start from scratch. Here, in a kitchen I created for a 1940s house, vintage-inspired profiles and timeless materials—soapstone and marble, zellige tiles, black-enameled metal, and white-painted wood—add charm to modern convenience.

MAKING SPACE

If you were to preserve the original purpose of every space in a historic home, you'd probably find yourself furnishing rooms just to collect dust. The drawing room. The parlor. The ballroom. Even without a conservatory or a billiard room, the floor plans of older houses can sometimes feel like a Clue game board—not particularly well suited for how we live now.

When I start a project, I like to remain open to rethinking what these most traditional of rooms might become and how they might function. It takes more than a little bit of imagination and energy, but it's worth it. The alternative—gutting a building entirely to create a completely new series of spaces—means sacrificing original detailing, character, and atmosphere you'll be hard-pressed to re-create. You end up losing much of what likely attracted you to the historic building in the first place.

Instead, I think about what *else* a room could be, often adding a second or even third purpose to a room type that contemporary living just doesn't require anymore.

The grand octagonal entry of my family's own townhouse, for instance, was unquestionably beautiful—but it was also quite formal feeling, and we had no real day-to-day use for a foyer of its size. Moving walls to make something smaller and better suited to our needs would have meant tearing out the remarkable and still largely intact 150-year-old plaster crown moldings as well as sacrificing the statement-making antique etched-glass skylight at the center of the space. Instead, we turned the octagon into a joint entryway, dining room, and library, with built-in bookshelves showing off our collection of vintage volumes and a small round center table for mail, keys, and bags that could expand to seat guests for dinner parties.

That, of course, is just one example. In the homes I design, butler's pantries become high-tech home offices, once-formal parlors become kid-friendly play spaces, and staff quarters become screening rooms. The ultimate goal is always to reimagine these rooms in ways that honor their origins while also ensuring they'll be well, and frequently, used today.

OPPOSITE: Our lives today often require great flexibility from the rooms in historic houses, even if their original architects and owners had different ideas about space and formality. I turned the large octagonal entryway of my own Boston brownstone into a multipurpose space that can serve as a foyer, a dining room, and a library, as needed.

RIGHT: What was once a second-level parlor in my townhouse is now a playroom for my daughters—and an atmospheric one, at that. **FOLLOWING PAGES:** I turned a similarly formal room in a shingle-style house into a family-friendly play space by combining elements both formal and informal—the window seat, center table, and leather poufs are particularly multifunctional. **PAGES 62–63:** Custom cabinetry painted a deep rich brown turned the den of my client's home into a lovely library, the glass doors showing off (and protecting) his extensive collection of antique books.

CONTEMPORARY ART

Adding artwork from the late twentieth century through today can bring a real freshness and currency to older homes. This is especially true in rooms that need a little nudge toward modernity to make their present-day occupants feel at home. While some interior designers like to use contemporary art to add a minimalist splash or a bold pop of color to traditional interiors, I generally avoid such high-contrast juxtapositions. Present-day works can provide a sense of excitement without shouting.

For my clients, I prefer to pull in pieces that whisper their contemporary credentials, especially photography and sculpture. I've found people relate to these two art forms easily—photography because it often represents an immediately recognizable world and sculpture because of its tactile qualities. Both do a good job of merging past and present.

The modern and contemporary paintings I gravitate toward share some of these qualities: they tend to be figurative, with highly textured brushwork and a style that combines Impressionism and Modernism. The works' moody, subtle colors echo the deep, rich palette I prefer. The pieces are clearly not from the nineteenth or early twentieth century—the dates of many of the houses I work on—but it's hard to tell exactly when after that they were made.

In the Beacon Hill townhouse I designed for committed Anglophiles, we turned to the work of British artist Tom Hammick, whose wooden pieces defy easy categorization. His wall-hung sculptures read as paintings, with a style that suggests the Impressionist, Modernist, and Surrealist movements all at once. The artist depicts relatively simple figures in landscapes that seem almost otherworldly. All of this made Hammick's work perfect for an interior that combined American with English and a few other global inspirations, and whose exact time period was intended to be hard to pin down. Timelessness and worldliness achieved.

OPPOSITE: Although much of the design and decor of this dining room pays homage to the house's English Arts & Crafts origins and details, I added a contemporary sculpture by Henry Moretti beside the fireplace. The weight of its forms and the expression of the natural mahogany grain work well with the vintage elements. **FOLLOWING PAGES**: In this Deco-inspired primary bedroom, I hung a textured piece by contemporary German artist Herbert Zangs over the sleek mid-twentieth-century bed by Silvio Cavatorta.

CUSTOM COMMISSIONS

I come across interesting, highly talented contemporary craftspeople all the time, and I love exploring their work and incorporating their pieces into projects. Doing so invites a greater variety of materials, textures, and styles into a space than would otherwise be there. In fact, these artisans often teach me what is possible, and expand my understanding of what might be, as we collaborate. Over the years, I've partnered with a henna artist to create motifs for hand-painted wall panels and worked with the designers at the British wallpaper source Fromental to produce panels with the look of embossed leather.

Like the modern and contemporary art I select for historic homes, the bespoke furnishings that I have made by local and international craftspeople don't usually look entirely of the moment, or even necessarily brand-new. I typically commission custom furniture, lighting, rugs, and fabrics to create something of a trompe l'oeil effect: I want to trick your eye into seeing something old where there's actually something new—or at least to trick it enough that it isn't sure what's old and what's new.

For example, I love sourcing incredible antiques, but there's often something about them that needs to be tweaked to make them right for the projects I'm working on, so that my clients can get the best use and most pleasure out of them in their homes. Custom commissions let me create, say, an Art Deco table in the exact size needed by homeowners. Fitting a vintage base with a top newly crafted at the right dimensions achieved just such a trick for the dining room of the Arts & Crafts home in the suburbs north of Boston. As far as most people know, the entire thing hails from the 1930s.

Bespoke furnishings are, by definition, custom-made; their uniqueness imbues them with a special quality that my clients very much appreciate. No one else has the same piece in their home, and they'd be hard-pressed to re-create it. This isn't about bragging rights—or, at least, it's not *just* about bragging rights. It's about knowing something has been created just for you, sometimes with your very own input, and always by the hand of a highly skilled artisan mindful of your needs and how you live right now.

OPPOSITE: I knew this dining room needed a table of rather specific dimensions, but I couldn't find an antique that fit the bill. Instead, I used an Art Deco base I loved and commissioned a new custom top for it that was the perfect size, creating a piece that had just the right look.

ABOVE: The British-accented kitchen in this townhouse features slightly overscale custom cabinetry—from a UK–based brand aptly called Plain English—that creates a welcoming sense of warmth and whimsy. We styled the pantry as a bright-green armoire. **OPPOSITE**: The look of the henna-inspired wall panels in the Concord living room would never have been possible without a bespoke commission.

THE HOUSES

AT HOME IN HISTORIC BOSTON

My first project in my new hometown of Boston—and one of the first interiors I designed on my own—was my own home. This 1850s Federal-style brownstone became a launching pad for my specialty of reimagining historic houses. And while it stands today as an object lesson in my studio's signature seamless mix of past and present, the house certainly didn't start out that way.

When my husband and I bought the second-floor apartment in the townhouse, my parents thought we were crazy—and they had no idea, nor did we, that we'd eventually buy the parlor floor, too, combining the two units into a single three-bedroom, 2,500-square-foot duplex. Back then, several of the building's once-grand spaces had been carved into tiny bedrooms, much of the original plasterwork had been stripped out, and many of the remaining details were in rough shape. But I could see past all that to recognize how this somewhat creaky, decidedly timeworn house could become a comfortable, timeless home for my family.

As with every project that's come along since this one, the existing interiors here had elements worth salvaging and others that weren't. Begging to be preserved and honored were the remaining acanthus leaf plaster moldings, the unique octagonal entry hall with its etched-glass skylight, the glazed-tile fireplace surrounds, and the incredible feeling of volume created by high ceilings. The mazelike arrangement of dark rooms in the back half of the house; the super saturated, stuffy-feeling Federal-era wall colors; and the 1980s-era Carrara marble tile floors all had to go, however.

After working with architect and contractor James Toris to reorganize the floor plan, opening it up to allow natural light to stream through the house from the street-facing front windows all the way to those overlooking the garden in the back, I began looking for ways to balance the house's

PREVIOUS PAGES: For the primary bedroom of my own home—in an 1850 brownstone in Beacon Hill, one of Boston's oldest neighborhoods—I had a Fendi chaise lounge recovered in an English flame stitch. The piece, which was one of the first items of furniture I ever purchased, always reminds me to hold on to furnishings that are special. You can always give them new life with fresh upholstery, paint, or other finishes. OPPOSITE: In my home's living room, I straddled the centuries, combining original ornate plasterwork with sleek Deco chairs, a late-twentieth-century Lucite table, a Victorian-style chandelier, and assorted family heirlooms and items collected on my own travels.

innate formality and sense of age. My goal was to add warmth, comfort, and a touch of contemporary style, making rooms that felt fresh and accessible out of spaces that might otherwise have seemed museum-like and off limits.

Wherever possible, I carefully preserved and restored the classical moldings and then painted them in the same colors selected for the walls, to allow the ornate plasterwork to recede a bit. I opted for darkly stained, random-width, hand-hammered oak flooring throughout, taking my inspiration from the original, relatively rough-hewn sub-floors—they felt right for the period even as they brought the formality quotient down. Hanging large, statement-making mid-century and contemporary light fixtures saved the ceilings from feeling too lofty while also adding modernity. (The living room got an antiqued Victorian-style chandelier dripping with crystals, but we added a heavy patina to the fixture to strike just the right balance.)

The house's color palette consists largely of subtle, moody hues that blend easily from one to the next, soothing the eye. When I needed brighter highlights, I borrowed hues from the blue-green and yellow fireplace tiles in the living room and primary suite. These tones seemed connected to Beacon Hill without being the traditional neighborhood palette of regal reds and royal blues.

As for materials, I looked to add a soft hand to formal lines: grass cloth above the paneled wainscoting in the primary bedroom; velvet on the cushions of a pair of bold, wood-framed Art Deco armchairs in the living room; wool and silk for the Tibetan-inspired custom carpets.

A worldly sensibility, together with my family's various collections of art and objects, provide the finishing touches. The combination keeps things interesting, while also conjuring a sense of comfort and a healthy dose of personality. Furniture—both vintage and new—comes from across Europe, and a button detail I noticed long ago in a Paris hotel adorns the top of the living room curtains. In nearly every space, you'll find a mix of my favorite things: West African busts, my grandparents' mid-twentieth-century paintings, pieces of Israeli metalwork, antique books bound in linen and leather, and turned-wood bowls—some of them made by my father's own hands.

OPPOSITE: Located just off the kitchen, my home office does very twenty-first-century double duty as a butler's pantry, styled as it might have looked 150 years ago. Custom built-ins maximize space, utility, and style. **FOLLOWING PAGES:** I designed the brand-new kitchen to look as if it had been there forever; like the office/pantry, it makes use of every square inch of buildable space—a necessity for city living.

ABOVE AND OPPOSITE: The kitchen's white oak open shelves echo the hue of the island and help break up an otherwise all-white wall of cabinetry. Custom metal-and-glass doors open to the garden. **FOLLOWING PAGES:** Original to the house, the yellow-glazed tiles of the primary bedroom's fireplace inspired the palette of hues I selected for the space.

OPPOSITE: My mother, who is an artist, made the pastel portrait that hangs in our primary bedroom. ABOVE: The primary bathroom's statuary marble, black-lacquered door, and polished-nickel hardware, mirrors, and wall lights imbue the space with a glamorous Art Deco atmosphere.

A CONCORD
ICONOCLAST

When I told the new owners of this 1940s home in historic Concord, Massachusetts, about my initial impressions of the property and my thoughts on what it could become, their reaction made me feel like fate had brought us together. At one of our very early meetings, we were talking about an area just off the entryway, a petite space that had originally been designed as a traditionally Colonial, Americana-style study paneled in knotty pine.

I mentioned I had an idea to turn the space into more of a cozy, sophisticated English country house library, and I began talking about borrowing an idea from a room clad with embossed leather panels at Boston's Isabella Stewart Gardner Museum. Before I could get very far, however, the clients interrupted to say they absolutely loved the Gardner—so much so that they had been patrons of the museum for years. I knew then that we couldn't have been a better match.

After that meeting, the layered, tactile, globally inspired, and stylistically agnostic aesthetic of the Gardner—a place that I, too, had long loved—became our touchstone. And Isabella Stewart Gardner herself

became our guide. An iconoclastic turn-of-the-twentieth-century collector of Italian Renaissance paintings, Asian and northern European art, and classical artifacts from antiquity, Gardner gathered ideas, objects, and inspiration from around the world. She bought what she loved, and she was absolutely fearless in the way she combined the pieces of her collection. In her museum, she wove together disparate threads to tell a story all her own, and all in a building somewhat inexplicably designed to resemble a Venetian palazzo. I saw a similar sense of worldliness and fearlessness in my clients. They had plenty of wanderlust, plus a bit of Gardner's colorful personal style, and they shared with me a willingness to experiment and change things up well beyond the bounds of tradition.

And this was a good thing, to be sure. Not least because, as traditional as it was, their home didn't offer much in the way of classical interior architecture for us to work with. Instead, there were low ceilings in the original part of the house, excessively high ones in a contemporary addition, and walls almost entirely devoid of ornamentation.

OPPOSITE: Walls clad with embossed leather panels in the Veronese Room at
Boston's Isabella Stewart Gardner Museum inspired my use of custom, hand-painted
wallpaper panels in the richly hued library of this 1940s family residence.

ABOVE: A timeless ivy-covered stucco facade—with its eight-over-eight windows, brick details, and patinated copper portico—helped me zero in on the largely European and British style influences of the interiors. **FOLLOWING PAGES:** I found the living room's antique Azerbaijani Tabriz carpet early in the project. Its vibrant colors and intricate pattern led me to select pieces with hues, motifs, and global influences to complement it.

The exterior, however, had character to spare and a distinct presence and patina. Seen from the street, the house and its gardened site looked far older than its eighty years. Beneath a low hip roof, ivy vines clung to the symmetrical facade, stopping only to reveal multipaned windows framed top and bottom by brickwork. In front of the main entrance, a pair of columns supported a gently curving, awning-like covering made of copper. The place might have been in England's Cotswolds—or grown out of Gardner's very own imagination.

Inspired by the charms of this exterior, plus my clients' sense of adventure and the example set by Gardner and her museum, I set about decorating.

Right away, I knew I would source furniture and accessories from around the world, creating a global mix of carefully crafted items that looked like they had been collected over time by someone with great, and highly eclectic, taste—just like Gardner. And so, in this house, you'll find a variety of mid-twentieth-century modern pieces from Italy and France keeping company with baroque-feeling shell-shaped English sconces, a fireplace surround clad with Portuguese azulejos tiles, an Art Deco Murano glass chandelier, a hundred-plus-year-old wooden Spanish side table with clean lines, and draperies lovingly hand-embroidered in Bhutan.

To make up for the home's lack of existing interior architecture, I clad nearly every wall with visually interesting materials, most artisanally made and internationally sourced. Each room got a unique treatment, but the richness of the textures and patterning, and a shared color palette, ensure everything coheres from one space to the next.

In that former study turned sophisticated library, I paid homage to the Gardner museum's embossed leather panels with a botanical pattern hand-painted in Hong Kong in deep, dark colors on thick parchment cut into rectangular sheets before being affixed to the walls. For the much lighter, brighter, and larger living room, I hired a henna artist to create motifs that were then transferred to abaca grass cloth and hung once again in panels, this time framed like artwork. The knotty pine walls of the main bedroom got a green-gray wash that let the grain show through, creating subtle stripes where the wood's edge took the stain differently.

These wall treatments sit with textiles and floor coverings that are just as full of texture, pattern, and character. Witness the library's fringed velvet sofa, deep-pile Moroccan carpet, and woven rattan valances from Atelier Vime in the South of France. Or consider the primary bedroom's agate-like carpet pattern, its bed hangings done in several different fabrics with global inspirations, its ruched-velvet Umbrian lampshades, and its linen curtains edged with a hand-embroidered trim from the United Kingdom. Meanwhile, the living room, despite its largely white walls, offers just as fulsome a visual feast, with block-printed floor-length drapes, velvet and nubby knit sofa upholstery, and a large antique Tabriz carpet from East Azerbaijan. Selected early in the process, that rug's combination of colors inspired the palette not just for this room but for the entire home.

That palette of variations on indigo blue and saturated vegetal hues—including aubergines and olives, tomatoey reds and oranges, and leafy greens and yellow golds—runs throughout the house, helping to harmonize what might have been a cacophony of disparate patterns and styles. Deployed differently, the colors cover nearly every surface from floor to ceiling in some spaces, like the library; while in others, such as the living room, they're used as subtler accents.

Together with all the various textures and bold patterning throughout, this palette unites the decor, creating a symphonic scheme whose overall effect is much more than the sum of its parts.

Gardner, I like to think, would approve.

ABOVE AND OPPOSITE: The house comprises an original 1940s structure and a later addition. I wanted the dining room, which is in the older section, to contain largely vintage pieces. In further homage to collector Isabella Stewart Gardner, I also wanted those items to come from around the world. Here, a 1940s Murano glass Ercole Barovier chandelier hangs over a French oak table from the same decade set with suzani-upholstered Danish Modern chairs by Henning Kjaernulf. The embroidered edge detail on the curtains hails from Bhutan.

A CONCORD ICONOCLAST

Once a somewhat staid, early-American study, this room emerged from its redesign as a library, with a distinctly British country house sensibility. It owes its sumptuous, sophisticated, comfortable appeal to the custom wallpaper panels, as well as its fringed velvet couch, fuzzy Moroccan carpet, and onyx-topped coffee table.

ABOVE: For the first-floor powder room, I commissioned a custom sink; artisans carved its scallop edge from a block of marble. Above it hangs a 1960s French rattan mirror and 1950s Stilnovo sconce. OPPOSITE: The entry's pale walls allow the striped hand-knotted Indian carpet on the stairs to claim the spotlight. Millwork painted aubergine—a color that connects all the surrounding rooms—echoes the rug's tones, while the open lines of a vintage bamboo side table and Empire-style cane chair keep the atmosphere as light and airy as the wall color.

A CONCORD ICONOCLAST

The primary bedroom borrows ideas from houses in the English countryside. Knotty pine millwork, stained a gray-green, provides a dreamy backdrop for layers of artisanally made Robert Kime fabrics in different, but related, textures, patterns, and hues. The plaster chandelier, reminiscent of the work of Alberto Giacometti, offers a modern note.

OPPOSITE: I found this romantic yet contemporary brass table lamp with a ruched-silk shade at a lovingly designed hotel in a centuries-old castle in the hills of Italy's Umbria. The hand-embroidered curtain trim hails from the UK. ABOVE: A French 1950s cerused oak desk by Guillerme et Chambron serves as a stylish workspace in the primary suite, where a custom, hand-knotted wool carpet suggests the fractal patterning of agate.

ABOVE AND OPPOSITE: The primary bath features bespoke Moroccan tiles in a geometric floor pattern inspired by a flatweave rug I saw in India. The global ideas continue with *tadelakt* walls, a 1950s Italian chair, a 1920s French Art Deco pendant, and a 1930s Murano glass Venini sconce. The soaking tub, from the Water Monopoly, was made in the UK.

BEACON HILL BRITISH

If you were sitting at the inlaid-birch Art Deco games table in the parlor of this Federal-style Boston townhouse—looking around at the richly layered, warmly whimsical, tailored but still comfortable decor—you could be forgiven for thinking you're in an ancestral manor house somewhere in the English countryside. And that's very much by design.

My clients here—longtime friends whose home is just around the corner from my own Beacon Hill brownstone—travel to the United Kingdom frequently, both for business and pleasure. Thanks to their trips, they developed a fondness not only for the look and feel of British interiors but also for a certain British way of living that somehow manages to feel formal, friendly, and familiar all at the same time. (There's always a certain casual atmosphere during a stay at an English country house hotel, even if it's black-tie for dinner.)

A married professional couple with two school-age children, my friends never quite told me they wanted a home in the English vein. But I knew that their affinity for the place is so ingrained into who they are, they would love this aesthetic direction. I also knew, however, that I was designing a four-story, 3,000-square-foot, almost impossibly narrow rowhouse in Boston for twenty-first-century living—not a sprawling neoclassical estate from the Victorian era in Buckinghamshire. I could work in an elevated British style, but I also needed to gently twist that vibe here and there. And so, I set about using the style and substance of one beloved international destination to imagine an interior that feels both of its actual place, and a bit globe-hopping, too.

The nineteenth-century house's Federal facade had landmark protection and needed to be preserved, but I had carte blanche on the interiors, which didn't retain much in the way of original historic detail anyway. This allowed me to reimagine both the overall floor plan and every element of each new room's ornamentation and decor, adding some decidedly English élan.

The British, I've found, have a different sensibility when it comes to color, pattern, and texture than we

OPPOSITE: Designing this Beacon Hill home for Anglophile clients who are also friends, I looked to UK–based brands when sourcing furniture, fabrics, and fittings—including the parlor's Soane wallpaper and antique English mantel. The particular layering of colors, patterns, and textures further recalls a British way of decorating.

do in the States. For as reserved as they can be—or at least as reserved as stereotypes suggest them to be—there's an exciting boldness to their way of designing: they use richer, deeper hues; they mix more prints; they highlight contrasting textures; and, always, they show off a willingness to layer, and in the most sophisticated way. A healthy dose of playfulness and whimsy, meanwhile, helps any potentially stuffy florals and chintzes feel more fresh than frumpy. Even younger people in England love them. And the same goes for antiques, which—perhaps thanks to the UK's longer history—seem to have nearly universal appeal there.

Great lovers of antique and vintage pieces, in addition to most things British, my friends were game to explore all of this with me, starting with bold color—and in particular my fondness for green. That became the hue that extends through the entire house, lending it something of a garden atmosphere. The greens are at their brightest in the Deco Moderne kitchen, which I finished using a UK-based cupboard maker aptly called Plain English. Things get lighter and moodier from there, shifting toward moss and olive in other spaces, such as the board-and-batten-clad dining room and the living room and parlor, where a variety of greens are set off against paler neutrals and deeper cognac hues.

The careful layering of complementary patterns in these spaces mirrors the mix of related colors. Consider the living room's upholstered chairs, which alone have two different prints on them. A pair of armchairs in the primary bedroom sit against pale, block-printed curtains and neutral walls covered in a textured paper and topped by Bordeaux-hued, half-round crown molding. At every turn, I selected for scale and tone to ensure that everything, no matter how layered, felt easy on the eyes.

I envisioned the cozy, clubby, and welcoming second-floor parlor as the most layered, and therefore most British, space in the house. Here, a vintage Kars rug from Turkey sits atop a larger sisal carpet, and the leafy vines of a botanical print climb the walls over molded wainscoting. Campaign-inspired metal-and-burnt orange leather chairs surround the antique Art Deco table between a tufted olive-green velvet sofa and an antique Georgian fireplace mantelpiece with a classically British fireplace fender. Nods to the New England setting include the antique Federal bull's-eye mirror over the mantel and the early American chest of drawers in the adjacent study.

I specifically—and almost exclusively—sourced furnishings from the UK for this project, something I wouldn't usually do. In addition to the Plain English kitchen, there are antique mantels and lighting from Jamb, wall coverings from Soane Britain, fabric from Robert Kime, and paint from Farrow & Ball. Most people who occupy these rooms wouldn't know all of this, of course, but the inherent Britishness of these items very much helps weave the design narrative together.

American pieces, meanwhile, provide a subtle tweak to the overarching English aesthetic, as do modern, global accents like the dining room's mid-twentieth-century Scandinavian chairs and the study's Swedish rug. Adding to the worldly mix, the study also features a rattan armchair and ottoman and a desk chair finished with a vintage Nigerian indigo textile.

Tom Hammick, the artist whose work I hung on large walls in both the living and dining rooms, also happens to be British, though the hard-to-pin-down style of his pieces transcends both place and time. He was a particularly perfect fit here, because that's exactly what I wanted this house to do as well.

OPPOSITE: In the living room, another mantel found in England keeps company with a wicker table on which sits a mid-twentieth-century ceramic lamp. The antiqued-mirror-clad chimneypiece contains a hidden cabinet for a television.

The house's patterns are perhaps no more layered than in the living room, where I used Indian block prints for the curtains and the paired chair and ottoman plus a cotton floral for the seats in the window bay. The rug's geometric motif and the sofa throw pillows' floral and concentric squares enhance the mix further, while the narrow color palette ensures all the patterns play well together.

ABOVE AND OPPOSITE: The homeowners gave me free rein to run with green, one of my favorite colors, throughout the house, and the hue appears in various shades and tones in nearly every room. I used a pale mossy iteration of it to lacquer most of the cabinets, the custom island, and the pair of pocket doors in the kitchen.

Done in rosy reds and pinks and creamy neutrals, the entryway and mudroom complement the green spaces nicely. **ABOVE**: In the former, a Natan Moss lamp tops a French nineteenth-century rosewood console. **OPPOSITE**: In the latter, I styled the storage to recall the luggage lockers you might see in a nineteenth-century London train station.

BEACON HILL BRITISH

Though not as explicitly British as the UK—sourced wallpaper and mantel—or such English classics as the fireplace fender and button-tufted velvet sofa—the parlor's vintage chairs by Cleo Baldon and the Art Deco table I found at an antiques store in London feel of a piece with the overall scheme.

ABOVE AND OPPOSITE: The saturated, verdant hue of the glossily painted
wet bar (above) echoes the deep green of the sofa in the adjacent parlor
(opposite), as well as the armoire-style pantry in the kitchen. Repeating a color
across different rooms in different ways—as an accent in one, washing it over
all the cabinets in another—helps a design scheme cohere beautifully.

OPPOSITE: The look-through from the wet bar reveals a global assortment of pieces in the study: a vintage Nigerian textile covers the chair behind a French Maison Franck desk, and a new Swedish rug covers the floor. ABOVE: I modeled the powder room's millwork on similar paneling I've long loved on the turn-of-the-twentieth-century storefronts of boutiques in Milan and Paris.

The glazed Moroccan tiles,
veined Breccia marble,
and stained cabinetry of
the primary bathroom
mine a narrow but rich
vein of the color spectrum
from merlot to mahogany
to toasted almond.
Unlacquered brass sconces,
fixtures, and cabinet pulls
complement the palette.

Although awash in pattern and texture, the primary bedroom remains a truly soothing space, thanks to the use of neutral hues both pale and deep. The twinned chairs, each upholstered with a pair of patterns, in front of the block-printed curtains feel especially British.

MEDITERRANEAN REVIVAL

Oftentimes, there's something about a historic building's particular period or style that can provide a pretty specific sense of what the reimagined interior should become. But other times, the existing architecture opens up a wide range of possibilities, inspiring the mind to wander more freely.

That was exactly the case with the redesign of this 1928 house in my hometown of Westport, Connecticut, just around the corner from where I grew up. Here, the building's aesthetic was surprisingly Mediterranean—a rarity in the area—which encouraged me to diverge from the more typical New England vernacular styles that define the surrounding neighborhoods. The almost storybook-like house presented a definite mix of southern European influences: it wasn't quite a Tuscan farmhouse nor a hacienda in Andalusia, not a Greek Isles getaway nor a South of France villa. It was none of those things exactly while also managing to contain a bit of each of them all at once. And

that—together with the freedom afforded me by the homeowners, a young couple with two sons in middle school—led the architect, Austin Patterson Disston, and me to create something truly special.

Approached through a set of metal gates, the L-shaped house has the feel of a timeless, old-world country estate almost before you even see it. A series of stone walls contain its three-plus acres, and terra-cotta roofs top its walls of New England fieldstone punctuated by deeply set windows, wooden shutters, and iron grates. The interiors we inherited, in contrast, felt decidedly American—and perhaps worse, late-twentieth-century suburban—as well as much darker and more compressed than they could have been.

My main goal was to add an additional layer of architecture throughout the house. I wanted each room to have as much character as that incredibly captivating exterior. In the sunken living room, that meant creating a series of salvaged wood ceiling beams and a custom-carved fireplace made of

OPPOSITE: To provide this 1920s Connecticut house with a greater sense of architecture, I added reclaimed wood beams to several spaces, including the dining room, where I had a decorative painter create a geometric design inspired by one I'd seen at a vineyard in Portugal. FOLLOWING PAGES: The Mediterranean-inspired exterior influenced many of my decisions for the interiors.

ancient limestone that had sat on the seafloor off the coast of Malta since the Jurassic Period. For the dining room, I designed a black-painted wood ceiling, its distressed and reclaimed beams hand-painted with a geometric motif spun from one I'd seen in a vineyard in Portugal. The primary bedroom got another painted and beamed ceiling, this one deep red, like the roof, while the entry got an open wet bar, the green glaze of its handmade Moroccan tile backsplash pulling from the verdant landscape seen through the windows. In the kitchen, we brought the warmth of stone inside, cladding the walls in local fieldstone that replicates the exterior, and nods to French and Italian country houses. We then complemented this with more ancient Maltese limestone for the sink and countertops.

To balance the boldness of these statement-making moments and materials, I kept the hand-plastered walls a soft white and the floors quite simple throughout, skipping crown moldings and base-boards to make the low ceilings seem higher. And I selected largely European furnishings—antique, mid-century modern, new, and custom—with clean, sculptural forms that would balance the somewhat ornamental elements of the new interior architecture. These relatively chunky pieces have a monumental, even monolithic presence, but a softness, too, thanks to their gentle curves and plush upholstery. The serene color palette, meanwhile, largely reflects the neutral, gradient earth tones of the stone exterior, with the occasional accent hues echoing the green gardens, red roofs, and blue sky and swimming pool.

If there's a certain sophisticated Mediterranean monastery look to the home, that's not unintentional. A desire for simplicity and spareness guided the airy aesthetic ethos here. As I mixed a broad array of elements past and present with plenty of Southern European globetrotting, I was careful to relate the new additions to existing details, material, and colors. In doing so, we managed to honor the house's origins and setting in ways that hadn't been celebrated in decades, while also making it brighter and more welcoming than ever before.

OPPOSITE AND FOLLOWING PAGES: Throughout the house, I chose furniture with a sculptural feel—akin to work by British artist Henry Moore. This is especially true of the pieces in the sunken living room, where a curving new sofa and cane-backed chairs flank a vintage arched lamp and a rectilinear Maison Jansen coffee table of brass and red glass. The custom fireplace is carved of limestone from Malta, and the photograph by Tina Barney is titled *The Two Students*.

LEFT: The dining room's vintage Ilmari Tapiovaara chairs sit at a Jordi Vilanova–inspired custom table beneath a mid-twentieth-century pendant. The art is by Robert Polidori.

FOLLOWING PAGES: Blending indoors and out, I clad the kitchen walls in the same New England fieldstone as the exterior. Vintage pendants hang above a reclaimed walnut island designed to look like a freestanding antique.

133

OPPOSITE: The base of the stairs—where a piece by Jonathan Cross sits on an Italian Art Deco side table from the 1940s—offers a sense of quietude. Though I don't usually design with white plaster walls, in this house they allow the sculptural furniture and the embellished ceilings to shine. **ABOVE:** Thanks to the cross vaulting of the ceilings, the artisanal joinery of white oak floors, and a Savonarola stool in between, the simple intersection of two upstairs hallways is another place for quiet repose.

OPPOSITE: With its geometric floor tile, Pompeiian-red lacquered vanity, and mirrored wall, the primary bathroom has a high-gloss, mid-twentieth-century feel, recalling the work of Italian designers of the period, not least Gio Ponti. ABOVE: I went graphic in the ground-floor powder room, where a brown-and-white checkerboard of Moroccan tile covers the floors and climbs the walls. The custom carved sink, like the living room fireplace and kitchen counter, is cut from Maltese limestone that had been at the bottom of the Mediterranean Sea for eons, making it impervious to stains. The pendant and mirror are vintage.

I'd seen a ceiling painted this particular red in a home in the Greek islands, and I thought it perfect for the primary suite here. The artwork above the bed is by Chilean painter Claudio Bravo.

ABOVE: An addition to the house—the lower roof lines in the foreground here, as well as the lower portion extending to the left—blends neatly into the architecture of the original 1928 structure. **OPPOSITE:** The sports barn, in a wing of the addition, serves not only as a space for athletic endeavors but also for large-scale entertaining.

ARTS & CRAFTS INSPIRATION

This 1904 English Arts & Crafts–style house just north of Boston might have ended up looking like a museum. Its gable-roofed, shingle-clad exterior and darkly stained, carved-wood interior details were so remarkably well preserved, they demanded attention, and they could easily have dictated the design of some rather weighty, period-perfect Arts & Crafts decor. Rooms filled exclusively with stolid brown furniture and William Morris prints were definitely not what my clients and I had in mind, however.

After many long conversations, we decided on a more complex, nuanced, and collected-looking scheme that would impart the house with some levity and a personality all its own. The idea was to provide balance to the existing design elements by adding a diverse array of furnishings in an assortment of styles. These would complement the original architecture without strictly adhering to the Arts & Crafts aesthetic.

To accomplish this, I sought out furniture, fabrics, fittings, and finishes that had enough visual interest and heft to hold their own against the original rich wood detailing. Whenever possible, I selected sculptural pieces that revealed the hand of the artisan who made them and celebrated the materials with which they were made—key principles of the Arts & Crafts movement. A palette of soft but saturated hues, tactile textiles, and largely nature-inspired prints served to soften some of the home's harder edges, as well as the previously harsh contrast between the ubiquitous dark wood and the original white walls we'd inherited. The result is a warm, welcoming, and comfortable residence that was exactly what my clients, a couple with three young children, wanted.

This inviting atmosphere makes itself manifest the moment you enter the house, as does the mix of styles and eras that complement the Arts & Crafts aesthetic. Here, the deep blue hues of an antique Kurdish rug lay the groundwork for a hospitable scene in which the scrolling forms of the original carved-wood stair rail sit well with two highly geometric pieces from the modern movement—a teak-and-cane Pierre Jeanneret Chandigarh chair and a

OPPOSITE: When reimagining a highly atmospheric 1904 home originally built in an English Arts & Crafts style, I had to carefully calibrate my scheme to spotlight some of its historic details and let others recede. In the entry, that meant painting the wainscoting and door trim white, while leaving the carved stair railing and paneled door stained. I then selected modern furnishings with a warmth and weight similar to the existing wood details.

mid-twentieth-century mahogany console, both of which celebrate their wood construction in the same way the stairs do.

The sculptural, largely wood furniture sourced from a range of eras, styles, and locations continues in the living room. There, every newly added piece needed to be as statement-making as the original woodwork, which extends from polished floor to heavily beamed ceiling. In the window bay, the strong forms of contemporary wood-and-rope chairs surround a monumental round table with a wide fluted base. In the center of the room, a custom sofa in a rich aubergine and angular 1960s Illum Wikkelsø wood-framed lounge chairs sit atop a highly textured Moroccan rug. An Italian chandelier provides lightness and another mid-century accent.

Color serves as a unifying element in the family room. Because of the space's somewhat confusing layers of paneling, moldings, and ceiling trims—all stained more darkly than anywhere else in the house—I painted almost all the existing woodwork with Farrow & Ball's Lulworth Blue, a color named after a cove in Dorset and used in many William Morris designs. When you have a room with challenging or even overwhelming interior architectural elements like these, choosing a single hue, especially a soothing one, can help calm everything down, and prevent your eye from bouncing all over. It also makes for a cozy atmosphere that was perfect for this snug, kid-friendly play and TV-watching spot. I found a velvet in a similar, darker hue to upholster a curving channel-tufted custom sofa and selected burgundy-glazed tiles for an inset accent in the original wood mantelpiece. Though not actually of the period, they feel just Arts & Crafts-y enough.

That "just enough" idea also defines the dining room, where I deployed a William Morris print for the wallpaper—selecting one whose subtle pattern and low-contrast, neutral hues whispered Arts &

Crafts instead of shouting it. This I paired with a complementary Rose Cumming pattern for the curtains. From there, I took a turn to the modern era: there's a richly grained wood Art Deco table, angular mid-twentieth-century-inspired chairs, a sideboard with interesting joinery, and a slightly industrial feeling metal-and-glass chandelier from one of my favorite contemporary makers, Apparatus. Each celebrates something unique about the artistry of the materials with which it's made as well as the careful craftsmanship of its construction—two Arts & Crafts hallmarks.

The kitchen is the project's pièce de resistance. Taking inspiration for its particular mix of materials and colors from the Art Deco period, I imagined what a luxed-up version of a below-stairs kitchen might have looked like at a grand countryside estate built in the 1920s. White hand-glazed tiles clad the walls, Arctic Gray marble tops the cabinets, and a custom brass-trimmed, black-enamel stove hood crowns the Lacanche range—all of which signal that this is a working culinary space. But the custom white oak cupboards, with their mix of painted and wood-grain finishes and patinated brass hardware, feel almost like fine antique furniture, and their complex crown moldings connect their aesthetic with the woodwork throughout the house.

This kitchen, which may well be my favorite room in the house, manages to depart more fully from the Arts & Crafts look than the other rooms. But its thoughtful use of material, texture, and color, as well as its artisanally made elements, ensure it remains integrated into the whole.

Like the rest of the interior   and, I think, like all the best twenty-first-century interiors in historic homes—the kitchen keeps people wondering what is old and what is new, what was original and what was recently added. It's this subtle sense of mystery that gives this house, and houses like it, personality and spark.

PREVIOUS PAGES: Painting the den's walls, trim, and ceiling the same moody shade of medium blue created a surprisingly neutral canvas onto which I layered pattern, texture, and sculptural furniture and lighting. ABOVE: A striated flatweave lends a cozy feeling to the stairs, as does the landing's mid-twentieth-century bench topped by an ikat pillow.

OPPOSITE AND ABOVE: The forms of the sculptural furnishings I selected hold their own against the muscular millwork. Throughout, I selected pieces whose materiality matched the Arts & Crafts ethos. In the living room, vintage cerused wood-and-rope chairs sit at a round table with a base that looks like a hefty fluted column. Flanking the contemporary bronze-and-brass coffee table are Illum Wikkelsø lounge chairs from the 1960s and a custom sofa, behind which sits a vintage Einar Johansen table lamp.

PREVIOUS PAGES: The dining room's William Morris wallpaper is the closest the decor gets to a direct Arts & Crafts echo. Picking a relatively muted pattern kept the reference subtle. Once again, the furniture's forms and artisanship—including the contemporary Apparatus chandelier—relate to the aesthetic's mindset. **OPPOSITE AND ABOVE:** Imagining the house's kitchen and butler's pantry were renovated in the 1920s or '30s, I created an Art Deco—inspired brass and black enamel hood to match the Lacanche range, complementing these with Arctic Gray marble counters and a backsplash whose subway tiles have a hand-glazed look.

ABOVE: Now enlarged, the primary bathroom features vintage Murano glass sconces and unlacquered brass faucets and cabinet pulls that will patinate beautifully. RIGHT: Warm textures, richly polished woods, and a judicious use of pattern turn the primary bedroom into a sanctuary. I especially love the vintage elements: in the window bay, an Italian chandelier from the 1950s hangs over a Wiener Werkstätte table I found in Vienna, and a Baguès lamp sits beside a bed from Leonards New England.

FORMALITY MEETS FUNCTION

Originally built in 1910, this house just west of Boston has an especially traditional, formal character. It overlooks the city from a lofty position on a small hill, surrounded by beautifully landscaped grounds bursting with an array of mature plantings. Stucco cladding and a red roof give the building a bit of a Mediterranean air, and neoclassical details confirm its classical old-world élan. That sensibility continues inside thanks to the fluted ionic columns, dentil moldings, and wainscoting of its spacious rooms. The property isn't quite palatial, but when I first saw it, I realized it had a certain grandeur that I wanted to celebrate—albeit in ways that felt appropriate to my clients.

The homeowners—friends I'd known for years—live well, and they love to entertain, both formally and more casually, for groups big and small. They saw this house as a place that would help them do all of that. So, together we worked out a concept that made room for their lifestyle: a refined but still warm and welcoming sensibility in the original parts of the house, where I skewed my schemes more classically, and a relaxed feeling in the contemporary-leaning rooms of a new, Art Deco–inflected, glass-walled extension that would be added off the back. In the end, this project may well seem more formal than any other I've done, but it is a formality defined by a look of lived-in luxury.

Take, for example, the entry. Here, I preserved all the original millwork—crown molding, wainscoting, pilasters, and tall baseboards, plus those fluted columns and dentil details—then paired a Biedermeier center table from the homeowners' collection with newly acquired Art Deco pieces: a glass pendant lamp, high-backed armchairs, and a custom faux-shagreen-wrapped credenza inspired by French 1930s mid-century designs. Underfoot, there is an antique Persian Malayer carpet. Though it could seem formal, this rug shows its age with some wear and fading. You don't feel like you're supposed to avoid standing on it.

OPPOSITE: Although the footprint of every other space in this Colonial-style home was changed, that of the living room remained in place, which allowed its neoclassical moldings, as well as its impressive fireplace, to be preserved in their entirety. I combined these formal historic fixtures with the contemporary lines of a bronze Cambodian rain drum used as a side table, a Stephen Antonson plaster lamp, and a custom wool and silk rug with a classical Greek key border.

A similar mix defines the dining room, also in the original part of the house, where I took inspiration from the entry's historic details to imagine wall paneling and ceiling details, then cut against any sense of stuffiness with a wavy, fashion-forward Missoni-style fabric in shades of green-blue for the chairs and a playful piece of contemporary art—one of Hunt Slonem's parrot paintings.

Enclosed by horizontally paned floor-to-ceiling windows that reference both Art Deco architecture and the long lines of the house's original facade, the new addition—whose exterior architecture is by LDa—holds more private, informal spaces. These include a family room, kitchen, and study. My goal here was to create an air of coziness that would still complement the refinement of the historic rooms. Throughout, I created layered moldings and millwork that, like the best Deco designs, could read as simplified versions of classical forms, with lower profiles and little in the way of ornate detail (no dentil here) yet still plenty of visual interest.

The textiles and other materials I used in the addition may not be quite as luxe as those of the older area, where, in the living room, for instance, a blend of antique and newly made seating covered in wool bouclé and cotton velvet sit on a silk carpet.

But the more casual linen upholstery of the low-slung, clean-lined contemporary sofa and the thick pile of the custom wool carpet—cut with a Greek key pattern for another nod to classicism—remain elegant enough to feel connected to that formal setting. At the same time, they let you know this space is for absolute comfort and relaxation.

Even with these rather different atmospheres—old and new, formal and relaxed—under one roof, the house holds together very well from one room to the next. This is thanks not only to the addition of casual elements in the most refined spaces and refined ones in the casual, but also to a unified palette of colors and materials that weaves its way around the entire house: soft and highly tactile textiles combine with rich but neutral earth tones accented by teal blues and greens both pale and saturated.

This house is a perfect example of how the decor of rooms can, and should, indicate their use: more refined living and entertaining in the more public formal-looking spaces, private relaxation in rooms that seem more comfortable. That's a lesson I've learned from historic houses—where there could never be any mistaking the main bedroom for, say, the maid's room—but it's one that often gets overlooked in homes today.

OPPOSITE: In the living room, a custom chesterfield—a traditional sofa made modern with bouclé upholstery—sits in front of a window wall accented by bespoke drapes with embroidered edge details. FOLLOWING PAGES: The room's generous proportions led me to use two coffee tables, one of them nesting, to have the flexibility to fill the center of the room further. The balanced furniture arrangement offers a visually engaging suggestion of symmetry, in keeping with the room's architecture, without creating a mirror image from one side to the other.

Because of its size and its original neoclassical details, the grand entry foyer demanded furnishings with gravitas. I hung a vintage French Art Deco chandelier by Atelier Petitot over a Biedermeier center table then added a custom mid-century modern—style console covered in shagreen and a pair of Deco armchairs.

OPPOSITE AND ABOVE: The underlying palette of pale, creamy neutrals blends well with deeper earth tones like walnut and cognac. The rich, saturated warmth of the wet bar's lacquered cabinets and Cipollino Fantastico marble gives way to a mix of light and dark tones in the dining room. There, the chairs upholstered with a wavy, Missoni-style fabric and the Hunt Slonem artwork hung over the console provide a bit of whimsy. I designed the motifs of the ceiling molding and mirror-fronted cabinet to complement each other.

The lines of the kitchen, which is located in an Art Deco—influenced wing newly added to the house, follow those of the windows' horizontal panes. This lets the custom cabinetry feel entirely of a piece with the architecture. The fluted glass panels in the upper cabinets and tiled walls add to the look.

ABOVE: I designed a custom hood of stainless steel and darkened brass to crown the statement-making Lacanche range and selected Macaubas Fantasy quartzite for the countertops. **OPPOSITE AND FOLLOWING PAGES:** The homeowners wanted the kitchen banquette, in a glass alcove, to be large enough to host informal dinner parties with friends, as well as family meals. A Deco-inspired Charles Edwards chandelier hangs above.

ABOVE: Located off the foyer, the powder room gets used mostly by guests when the homeowners entertain. The metallic marbleized wallpaper, glossy woodwork, vintage Murano glass mirror, and faceted custom pendant make sure the space sparkles during parties.
OPPOSITE: The family room acts as a bridge between the formal, public part of the house (the living room, seen in the background) and the casual (the kitchen, just off camera to the left).

Since the family room is in the new wing of the house, it skews modern, while rooms in the original 1910 portion are more classically minded. Moldings in this space are spare compared to those of the living and dining room, and the furniture is more sculptural and clean-lined.

ABOVE AND OPPOSITE: I designed the primary bedroom—which sits high in the hilltop home, enjoying prime treetop views—as the most soothing of all of the house's serene spaces. A low-contrast palette of creams and blues combines with subtle patterning and soft natural textures to create a cocooning feeling. A capiz shell pendant globe serves as a focal point in the high vaulted ceiling.

LEFT AND ABOVE: The primary suite's vaulted ceilings continue in the light-filled bathroom. Here, the geometric motif of the mosaic floor mirrors the chamfered edge of the wall moldings and vanity cabinetry. The Sputnik chandelier above is a 1960s piece by Richard Essig.

PREVIOUS PAGES AND ABOVE: Windows enclose the study on three sides, opening it to the garden and abundant sunshine. (The crown molding conceals shades in recessed pockets.) The furniture mix includes a vintage Kars rug and klismos chairs. OPPOSITE: The study occupies a 1970s addition to the house—seen in the foreground—to which columns were added to make the structure look like an enclosed porch. Beyond, the new Deco-influenced addition steps back, following the footprint of the original house. Its glass walls help it all but disappear into the landscape.

FORMALITY MEETS FUNCTION

SHINGLE-STYLE CHIC

It would be going a touch far to say that a historic house could ever give me *too* much to work with, but this one came pretty close.

This 1880 shingle-style structure in a secluded enclave of the Boston suburbs had changed hands only a few times over its many years, and it had been remarkably well preserved along the way. The house practically overflowed with character-rich details—beautiful stained-wood moldings, paneling, and built-ins; a charming covered front porch; third-floor dormers; and a central Palladian window, not to mention an adorable alcove on the stair landing designed as an in-house telephone booth. Though the building had an almost cottage-esque appearance from the front, inside it offered a generous sense of space, with plenty of square footage, and more than ample acreage outside, all of it arranged in a way that remained well suited to contemporary living and entertaining both indoors and out.

These all seemed like assets, and they were, to be sure. But, at the same time, much of this made the unquestionably gracious house feel overly grand, dark, and, well, old for its new owners—a young couple with a toddler and a baby on the way.

My project here, then, became a quest to create a more youthful, comfortable, family-friendly scheme that played to the strengths of the impeccably maintained property even as it dialed down the grandeur. I saw the house as a gift, and I wanted to make sure we used it wisely.

For me, this meant keeping the original architecture intact, including nearly all of the darkly stained woodwork, then layering in elements that would add freshness and levity: brighter colors, softer textures, sculptural lighting, global inspirations, and patterned accents.

The expectation for the interiors of a house like this is often for a continuation of the exterior—more shingle-style furniture, a classically New England palette of wispy blues and greens, floral prints, overstuffed upholstery. Such traditional decor, however, would have made the architecture here seem like too much: too heavy, too antique, too

OPPOSITE: Set in a particularly picturesque part of Massachusetts, this 1880 shingle-style house offered atmospheric, pitch-perfect period details aplenty. Its double parlor felt somewhat large for its twenty-first-century owners, however, so I turned the bay in the background into an inviting nook perfect for games, homework, and tea or coffee.

formal. And that was exactly the opposite of what the house needed—and what my clients, who had a casual streak and a contemporary bent, wanted.

One of the first things I remember the homeowners telling me when we started working together was that they weren't afraid of color. They were ready to be daring and bold in their choices. And that was good news to me. It led me to select hues and tones that could withstand all the dark woodwork and make a statement all their own.

Because the stained, polished moldings and millwork had a bit of a masculine feeling, I went with relatively bright jewel tones that could skew more feminine. These hues weave their way throughout the home, especially the first floor. Extending an overall color palette across a house's many rooms like this allows each space to feel connected to the rest, which creates a soothing atmosphere. And simultaneously tweaking the palette to create different versions or variations of the same colors in different rooms adds a sense of novelty and even surprise as you move through the house. In this case, the emeralds, aquamarines, jades, corals, and sapphires I selected are at their deepest in the living room, used to swath the upholstered furniture, and appear in softer variations in other rooms.

The clients' request for a more contemporary look led me to avoid pattern almost entirely. Instead, I used layers of texture to provide visual interest while softening the strong architecture and balancing the heavy woodwork. I began by adding tactile materials to many of the walls: grass cloth in blue-green for the dining room, ecru in the main bedroom, and a block-printed mustardy hue in the family room.

In the living room, I used a paper-backed linen in a barely there bone hue on the walls, then layered in even more softness with plush upholstery: Raw-silk pillows with piped edging top a button-tufted velvet chesterfield sofa, and linen and mohair pillows pile on another couch, this one covered in cotton. More velvet swaths the armchairs, and there's more tufting on the leather ottoman. To keep things from feeling too plush, I added craggy ceramic vessels on the mantel and Brutalist-style table lamps whose bases are comprised of hand-hewn nuggets of brass.

This house's wonderful sense of space and generous floor plan meant I didn't have to move any walls around to make the house better suited to a twenty-first-century lifestyle—and that let us preserve all the wonderful original architectural details. But I did still need to help my clients discover new, present-day uses for some of the existing spaces. What had once been a serious-feeling office on the second floor became a more whimsical family room and kids' play space, for example, and a window bay in the large living room that easily could have gone unused became an inviting games nook.

At every turn, I looked to leave plenty of room for children to run around, and I selected family-friendly furniture—a zinc-topped table, woven-rush chairs, galvanized-metal counter stools—that felt relaxed, easy to be around, and largely indestructible, even in the living and dining rooms. Solutions like these allow the house to feel as comfortable for my clients today as it did a century and a half ago for the no-doubt much more formal owners who built it.

OPPOSITE: The window bay centers on a custom games table based on a Deco piece I'd seen, its curves and angles echoed by the barrel-backed chairs and faceted pendant above. Built-in window seats in older homes can go unused; placing the table here helps overcome that challenge.

EARTH FROM ABOVE

PREVIOUS PAGES AND OPPOSITE: Deep jewel tones, including emerald, coral, and garnet, plus soft, cozy materials like velvet, mohair, and cotton, imbue the main living area with a cosseting richness.
ABOVE: A trio of blown-glass vessels, in various shades of amber, catch the sunlight.

OPPOSITE: The foyer extends the length of the house, enjoying lovely sun from windows in the front and back doors and at the top of the stairs. Painting much of the existing woodwork a stony off-white, I kept the scheme here light and bright to match. **ABOVE:** Marbleized wallpaper by Robert Crowder & Co. and a mid-century Egon Hillebrand mirror lend drama and a healthy dose of modernity to the powder room, which retains its original sink and wainscoting. **FOLLOWING PAGES:** The relatively pale hues of the dining room's furniture, as well as the steel blue horsehair wallcovering, prevent the original woodwork from feeling too heavy—especially important in this room, which doesn't get much sun and is used mostly at night.

ABOVE, OPPOSITE, AND FOLLOWING PAGES: The two sides of the kitchen—cooking and dining—sit in pleasant aesthetic dialogue thanks to subtle repetitions and a strong sense of balance. The dark zinc-topped trestle table—an indestructible piece, much appreciated by clients with children—recalls the soapstone counters; the neutrally hued linen roman shades echo the natural rush seats and backs of the chairs; and the galvanized steel counter stools are similar in tone to the cabinet and drawer pulls.

SHINGLE-STYLE CHIC

The primary bedroom's button-tufted headboard and contemporary lamps offer complementary contrast to the traditionalism of the paneled wainscoting and the prominent crown molding, with its dentil details. The boldly graphic classical motif on the embroidered Holland & Sherry pillows helps connect old and new.

MODERN FEDERALISM

Although my own nineteenth-century Beacon Hill townhouse came with plenty of original plaster moldings and carved millwork, many of the others in the area have a considerably more subtle aesthetic—one whose restraint I happen to admire just as much. The simplicity of the Federal-style brick exteriors of these buildings continues into their interiors, where clean lines and cozy spaces dominate. Found clustered together, often on some of the narrowest of Boston streets, these homes have a charming carriage house or mews aesthetic that can be just as captivating and inspiring as the grandeur of their more ornate cousins. And they come with none of the risk that an overabundance of ornamentation will make the house feel too grand for the way people want to live today.

In the case of this 1836, multistory rowhouse, its new owners had a more modern, contemporary-leaning aesthetic themselves, and so the relative minimalism of the building's original exterior Federal architecture very much appealed to them. The floor plan, however, did not. It had the kitchen in the low-ceilinged, semisubterranean garden level and a warren of too-small rooms on the floors above. None of it would work for this young couple and their growing brood of kids.

Together, we decided to take the house down to the studs—and beyond, really. I entirely reconfigured the floor plan to create a series of amply sized spaces on each floor that would flow easily from one to the next. That's especially important in a rowhouse like this that only has windows at its back and front, because it allows sunlight to penetrate all the way through the space. The entire second floor, for instance, became the primary suite, and at street level, I conceived an open kitchen and living area that would draw you in as soon as you entered the six-panel front door.

That front door and the molding and wainscoting flanking it, as well as the fluted framing and rosette corner blocks around the windows nearby, were the only original interior architectural features left in the house, the rest having been ripped out by the previous owners decades ago. I used them to guide my design for new detailing throughout. The crown moldings, baseboards, wall panels, and other

OPPOSITE: Clean lines, solid colors, boldly graphic patterns, and just the right amount of luster and polish give this reimagined mid-nineteenth-century Federalist townhouse a much-needed dose of twenty-first-century vitality, even as its look remains grounded in the classics.

elements I conceived all feature similar rectilinear motifs with fairly shallow, but still layered, profiles. That lets them dovetail nicely with the rigor and simplicity of their historic context.

These motifs repeat from the kitchen cabinetry, where I rendered them in white-painted wood, to the patinated bronze fireplace surround, to the lower-level family room, where I finished the floor-to-ceiling white oak paneling with a light stain to show off its beautiful graining. They even appear in the powder room, where I upholstered the lower part of the walls in leather with inset rectangles of nailhead studs to echo the look of wainscoting.

A house this narrow (it's only nineteen feet wide) and with this many levels (there are five) required considerable thought when it came to vertical circulation. I knew the home's central staircase needed to make a statement, but it had to be a smartly subtle one. You would be able to see it from practically everywhere in the house, and my clients would be spending a lot of time going up and down it. It had to be aesthetically interesting without completely stealing focus.

I once again turned to the street level's original window moldings for inspiration, borrowing their subtle but stylish fluted motif for the design of translucent ribbed-glass panels inset in bronze framing like that around the fireplace. This divides the stairs from the kitchen and living area while also letting in natural light. As the steps climb through the house, the paneling gives way to black lacquered railings and balustrades tipped with brass accents.

I repeated the black lacquer from the stairs in the street-level powder room moldings, adding a graphic marble mosaic floor in black, white, and gray. In the living area, primary suite, and lower-level family room, I swapped out traditional, almost Colonial-looking wooden mantelpieces for more monumental ones with strong but spare silhouettes in earth-toned marbles with painterly veining. The mantels almost look like they could have come out of Villa Necchi Campiglio, architect Piero Portaluppi's 1930s Art Deco masterpiece in Milan.

The home's narrowness (and subsequent lack of light) required me to think light and bright when it came to the color and material palette. I used much more white on the walls, and more high-gloss paint overall, than I might typically, and I chose metals, marbles, mirrors, and glass, as well as plush textiles like raw silk, velvet, and waxed linen, all with enough sheen to ensure the sun would bounce around everywhere.

The final result reflects who my young, stylish clients are—and how they want to live today—while also responding to the house's history. Grounded in the classicism of the Federal style, and the elegance that comes with that, these interiors now have an elevated, sleek, and sophisticated aesthetic that still manages to be comfortable, unfussy, and surprisingly kid-friendly. Fabrics and rugs are tougher than they look, and almost every surface wipes clean. These rooms can stand up to the wear and tear of daily use—and they need to.

My clients are now a family of five, and I know they make the absolute most of every single square inch of space in their home. And that is one of the greatest compliments any interior designer can receive.

OPPOSITE AND FOLLOWING PAGES: On the garden level, the family room's cerused white oak paneling offers extra warmth and lightness to a partially subterranean space, as do the overstuffed furnishings upholstered in rather bright colors using fabrics with the softest of textures.

ABOVE AND FOLLOWING PAGES: The original paneling of the door and surrounding wainscoting inspired the look of the cabinetry in the open kitchen and living area—a former double parlor that serves its contemporary family much better in this configuration. **OPPOSITE:** The house has five stories, so its owners spend a lot of time going up and down. To make the staircase feel special, I offered a glamorous Deco note: black-lacquered railings with custom brass fittings.

MODERN FEDERALISM

OPPOSITE: As a mother of two, I always like to combine whimsy and sophistication in children's bedrooms. Doing so helps a space grow with your kids. Here, the surprising colors of the faux bois wallpaper and velvet-upholstered bed provide a playful jolt. **ABOVE:** In the primary bathroom, platinum-hued travertine tiles play nicely with the brass details of the glass sconces by Ralph Lauren and the riveted mirror frame.

LEFT: Brass makes another primary suite appearance in the windowed dressing room, where the closet and drawer pulls echo the finish of the antique Federal-style bullseye mirror.
ABOVE: A sink cantilevered from the wall—with no vanity or other base beneath it—allows the graphic, geometric floor pattern to show itself off across the entire powder room.

The primary bedroom's travertine fireplace echoes the stone used in the tiles of the en suite bathroom and simultaneously recalls the silhouette of the mantel in the den. Subtle repetition across an entire house is the best way to make a scheme feel connected from one room to the next, with slight variations in a consistent palette of colors, shapes, patterns, and materials adding interest.

218

ISLAND BEAUTY

I'm in the lucky position of getting to design the interiors of houses that have history to spare, and with that history usually comes a built-in story—if not many stories. There are the narratives suggested by the hundred-plus-year-old architecture, others discovered about real-life previous owners, and still more based on imaginary characters who might have lived there decades or even centuries ago.

Newer buildings, especially ones with relatively nondescript architecture, rarely whisper sweetly in my ear. Instead, they can be almost perfectly silent. That certainly was the case, at least at first, with this house, a small, nondescript mid-twentieth-century ranch on Martha's Vineyard, just off the coast of Cape Cod. But the property did eventually speak to me—so much so that we bought it, and I took it on as a project, finally getting to own a little piece of an island that my husband and I had been coming to for decades and had grown to love.

Here, it wasn't historic architecture or artisanal design that grabbed my attention and inspired my creativity. The house had neither. Instead, it derived its character from its uniquely impressive setting.

The house sat on lightly wooded land in the island's pastoral West Tisbury district, away from the bustle of the Vineyard's busier towns and within view of the water. Most enticingly, the property included a private beach—a true local rarity—accessed by a sandy footpath through the backyard.

I knew almost right away that even though the house didn't suggest much, its setting did. If the house was a blank slate, the location was practically a completed canvas. It immediately conjured visions of a relaxed, casual coastal retreat with decor that pulled ideas from seaside destinations around the globe. The spare, straightforward cottage felt like it could have been on a beach anywhere. And that freed me to create an entirely transportive getaway that borrowed as many ideas from the coasts of Mallorca, Mykonos, and Mozambique as from Massachusetts.

Unlike most of the houses I work on, here nothing was precious, nothing had to be salvaged and preserved. But the more I looked at it, the more the low-lying house's existing architecture started to appeal to me. In the simplicity of its gabled rooflines, rectangular forms, and flowing open plan

OPPOSITE: This waterside home on the Massachusetts island of Martha's Vineyard combines coastal aesthetics from around the globe, juxtaposing the natural textures of bamboo and rattan, raw wood, and woven rope, jute, and cane.

with a guest wing and sleeping loft, I saw a beautiful but low-key bungalow, one whose casual, barefoot-chic beach vibe could be drawn out largely by reimagining all the surfaces and finishes—no gut renovation required. When I first saw it, the house had a certain suburban tract home quality to it; I wanted to give it new life as a contemporary-cool surf shack that would harmonize serenely with its seaside setting.

I started the house's reinvention from the outside in. I traded out a green asphalt roof for cedar shakes and replaced the exterior walls' white shingles with modern-feeling vertical planks of reclaimed cypress weathered to a warm gray. (This humble abode was never going to be one of the grand, whitewashed nineteenth-century whaling captain's homes you find elsewhere on the island.)

Driftwood hues like those on the exterior made their way into the interior. There, earthy, largely neutral, natural materials left in their purest state define the soothing, organic look and feel. I used more reclaimed cypress for the kitchen cabinet doors, to frame out doorways and openings from one room to the next, and to reclad existing ceiling beams. A trip to Morocco inspired my use of *tadelakt,* a limestone plaster with a somewhat mottled finish, on the walls of the kitchen and bathrooms. I complemented these walls with warm white concrete floors throughout the house.

This quiet palette of wood and plaster left me with a clean, light, and bright envelope that I filled with antique and vintage finds from around the world, all of them crafted of natural, often woven materials with nautical appeal. For the living room, I found a curvaceous mid-century bamboo chair, diamond-patterned sisal rug, and vintage cerused-oak and rope seats. In the adjacent dining room, Pierre Jeanneret–inspired chairs with cane seats and backs surround the table under a basket-like light fixture. A woven pendant light hangs over a woven-rope bed in a guest bedroom. To complete the decor, I added artisanal architectural details with a global feel, such as the hand-carved pyramidal motif of that bedroom's wood crown molding, which I'd seen in a private home in Marrakech.

I don't usually get to hear from the past owners of houses I redesign, but in this case I did. The man we bought it from—who'd used it for decades as part of a family compound, along with homes on several other adjacent properties—saw pictures of it and reached out with the kindest thoughts. He told me the house had special meaning to his family; it had long been the place they'd convene and relax in an incredible natural setting. Seeing what I'd done, he almost couldn't believe the transformation, but he was also thrilled by it. He appreciated the fact that the house could now have this unexpected second act.

Most people would probably have knocked it down and just started over—and, indeed, that's what happened to the similar houses nearby that had made up the rest of the family compound. But I saw this property with different eyes. I wanted to find a way to allow it to become a better, present-day version of itself. I think that's what was so pleasing to the previous owner and what ultimately made this reinvention successful.

OPPOSITE: Repainting the nondescript mid-twentieth-century bungalow's walls white and the new concrete floors a warm ivory elevates the architectural envelope while also letting the sculptural furniture enjoy the spotlight.

PREVIOUS PAGES: In the entryway, which affords views of the surrounding woodland, vintage cerused oak and rope chairs flank a rustic painted console I found at a flea market.
LEFT AND ABOVE: With its *tadelakt* walls and counters, rough-hewn woodwork, and range of ceramic and woven accessories, the kitchen borrows from the visual traditions of Morocco, Greece, and the coast of East Africa.

I based these custom beds on a pair of French 1950s rattan pieces I'd fallen in love with. They share a mid-twentieth-century Scandinavian modern nightstand and a ceramic lamp.

ABOVE: I turned a vintage Chinese table into a bathroom vanity by topping it with a hand-chiseled stone vessel, another flea market find. The 1950s rattan-framed mirror is French. OPPOSITE: A trip to Marrakech turned me on to the sort of geometric crown molding I designed for this guest bedroom, where vintage modern nightstands sit on either side of the bed and a contemporary pendant light hangs above.

LEFT: In the primary bedroom, a global assortment of woven artisanal items—including a Moroccan rug and blanket and Indian chik blinds—warm up the existing architecture. A wooden vase turned by my father sits beside a vintage leather and wood chair from Brazil.
FOLLOWING PAGES: The petite, spare house went from bleak to surf-shack chic thanks to reclaimed cypress boards installed vertically on the exterior.
PAGES 236–7: The property's hidden private beach—a Vineyard rarity.

NINA FARMER INTERIORS

I LOVE YOU MOM AND I WILL ALWAYS BE THERE FOR YOU QUINN

To Nina,
Here's to calm and inspiration. Best, A

colette 28

Hi Nina!
At long last, here is the march issue with your gorgeous home in it. Hope you're as happy with the feature as we were. Let's keep in touch—
v Noretta

House Beautiful

Nina

ACKNOWLEDGMENTS

The work showcased in this book wouldn't have been possible without the help, guidance, and wisdom of family, friends, colleagues, partners, and mentors too numerous to name here—but I can try. First and foremost, I want to thank my husband, Michael, who has been there through every moment of my career, supporting me through it all, and my children, Quinn and Colette, who inspire me every day with their clever minds and creative spirit.

There are not enough words to express my appreciation and love for my parents, who instilled in me a deep passion for the arts and for architecture from an early age. Long before I realized it myself, they noticed I had the skills and creativity to follow what would eventually become my chosen career path. I will be forever grateful for their teachings and their foresight.

Thank you, as well, to my clients: the homeowners who invite me to share the stewardship of their historic houses and allow me to play a part in shaping the future of these residences. Interior design is a deeply personal practice and process. The best results are born out of true collaboration, and I've been lucky enough to enjoy incredible partnerships with my clients.

It takes a team to design and implement every project. The members of my staff, both past and present—Isabel Brewster, Lindsey Nardolillo, Sydney Clapp, Brittney Lombardo, and Ariadna Cohen—demonstrated, and continue to demonstrate, a dedication to detail that has become a hallmark of our studio.

I have had the privilege of working with the most brilliant architects, contractors, craftspeople, and artisans over the years. Thank you all for joining me on this journey in pursuit of excellence and for executing every detail I designed with perfection. I want to extend special appreciation to the late James Toris, the architect and contractor with whom I partnered on some of my favorite projects, including my own home. You are sorely missed, both as a friend and a talented collaborator.

The photographers whose images are featured in this book—Stephen Kent Johnson, Jared Kuzia, Michael J. Lee, David Mitchell, Eric Piasecki, Paul Raeside, Eric Roth, and Lesley Unruh—make my work look its best, artfully capturing each room with the most beautiful lighting and angles. The expert, skilled eyes of interiors photography stylists Michael Reynolds and Mieke ten Have elevated every space seen in these pages.

I knew writer and editor Andrew Sessa intuitively understood me and my work from our first meetings, when he interviewed me for articles in 1stDibs' *Introspective* magazine and then again for *Architectural Digest*, where he dubbed me "the historic house whisperer." Interior design is such a visual language for me, and I can't think of anyone better to put what I do into words than him. Many thanks, as well, to graphic designer Celia Fuller, who understood my vision for this book from the very beginning and then spun that into a reality better than I could have ever imagined.

Finally, I want to say thank you to editor Kathleen Jayes and publisher Charles Miers at Rizzoli. They believed in my work and my approach, and then offered me the opportunity to create a book that would share it with all of you. Their support, and yours, means the world to me.

First published in the United States of America in 2023 by
Rizzoli International Publications, Inc.

300 Park Avenue South
New York, NY 10010
www.rizzoliusa.com

Copyright © 2023 Nina Farmer
Text: Andrew Sessa
Foreword: Mitchell Owens

PUBLISHER: Charles Miers
SENIOR EDITOR: Kathleen Jayes
DESIGN: Celia Fuller
PRODUCTION MANAGER: Barbara Sadick
MANAGING EDITOR: Lynn Scrabis

PRINTED IN SINGAPORE

2023 2024 2025 2026 / 10 9 8 7 6 5 4 3 2 1

ISBN: 978-0-8478-7350-0

Library of Congress Control Number: 2023934722

Visit us online:
Facebook.com/RizzoliNewYork
Twitter: @Rizzoli_Books
Instagram.com/RizzoliBooks
Pinterest.com/RizzoliBooks
Youtube.com/user/RizzoliNY
Issuu.com/Rizzoli

PHOTOGRAPHY CREDITS

STEPHEN KENT JOHNSON: 1, 10, 23, 28, 45, 47, 49, 60-61, 125-143, 186-203, back cover
JARED KUZIA: 2, 29-37, 48, 53, 62-63, 66-67, 70, 105-123
DAVID MITCHELL: front cover, 3, 12, 18-19, 54, 71, 86-103, 238
PAUL RAESIDE: 8, 20, 46, 57, 64, 69, 72-85, 144-157
LESLEY UNRUH: 15, 58-59
MICHAEL J. LEE: 16, 26-27
ERIC PIASECKI: 24-25, 38, 42-43, 158-185, 204-218
ERIC ROTH: 40, 221-237